TRANSLATING AIR

THE HUGH MACLENNAN POETRY SERIES

Editors: Allan Hepburn and Carolyn Smart

TITLES IN THE SERIES

Translating Air

Kath MacLean

McGill-Queen's University Press

Montreal & Kingston • London • Chicago

"The Master (section III)" by H.D. (Hilda Doolittle), from *Collected Poems, 1912–1944,* © 1982 by The Estate of Hilda Doolittle. Reprinted by permission of New Directions Publishing Corp.

ISBN 978-0-7735-5456-6 (paper)
ISBN 978-0-7735-5523-5 (ePDF)
ISBN 978-0-7735-5524-2 (ePUB)

Legal deposit third quarter 2018
Bibliothèque nationale du Québec

Printed in Canada on acid-free paper that is 100% ancient forest free (100% post-consumer recycled), processed chlorine free

Funded by the Government of Canada

Financé par le gouvernement du Canada

Canada Council for the Arts

Conseil des arts du Canada

We acknowledge the support of the Canada Council for the Arts, which last year invested $153 million to bring the arts to Canadians throughout the country.

Nous remercions le Conseil des arts du Canada de son soutien. L'an dernier, le Conseil a investi 153 millions de dollars pour mettre de l'art dans la vie des Canadiennes et des Canadiens de tout le pays.

Library and Archives Canada Cataloguing in Publication

MacLean, Kath, author
    Translating air / Kath MacLean.

(The Hugh MacLennan poetry series)
Poems.
Issued in print and electronic formats.
ISBN 978-0-7735-5456-6 (softcover). –
ISBN 978-0-7735-5523-5 (ePDF). –
ISBN 978-0-7735-5524-2 (ePUB)

I. Title. II. Series: Hugh MacLennan poetry series

PS8575.L427T73 2018   C811'.54   C2018-903247-2
                                            C2018-903248-0

This book was typeset by Marquis Interscript in 9.5/13 New Baskerville.

Frontispiece: Man Ray, *Hilda Doolittle*, 1925. (National Portrait Gallery, Washington, DC, AS./NPG.77.84.1)

For Chelsea, every moment was a gift –

CONTENTS

how could he have known
how each gesture of this dancer
would be hieratic?
words were scrawled on papyrus,
words were written most carefully,
each word was separate
yet each word led to another word,
and the whole made a rhythm
in the air,
till now unguessed at,
unknown.

H.D., *A Dead Priestess Speaks*,
from "The Master," Part III, *Collected Poems*, 454.

I

Fiery Moments

LAST TRAIN TO WYNCOTE

Climbing into the crow's nest
we watch the last train to Wyncote jolt past.
Dryad, he says, *there is no other.*

Again, I am mistaken.
I had slipped day into a poem
I was having trouble writing.

Ray wanted to imagine confusion
but I had no image for it. The wind
blew about the branches, & the tree shifting
its gaze blinked into the sun.
I was mistaken.

There was no such thing as time;
it was afternoon, too early
for mother to call us in by the side door,
much too early for a restless leaf rubbing
another notch in the trunk's groove.

In our nest above the trees I wanted
simplicity, but confused it with love's wet kiss,
the breathless pause of practicality.

Dryad, he chirped, *this is the last train.*
I was mistaken. Writing love
in the afternoon; is it rapture,
is it bliss?

Confuse a poem for an image that cares
what time it is, he said,
what slender birds –

Mistaken, again. I had not recognized
simplicity. It was much too
early –

I had no image for it.

YES, THEY MUST HAVE BEEN BLOSSOMING APPLE-TREES

Yes, they must have been blossoming apple-trees
when he read William Morris, poems swelled
in the sun, flickering fortunes, hieratic dreams.
The possibilities seemed endless.

Days grew, seasons seeded
long days of blossoms not-yet-
bloomed. Just
then, the world changed.

He was, I think, always
enchanted by brilliance, & I was,
I think, easily charmed.

Im-posing, he scribbled in his little *Book of Dreams*,
weaving the words: *Usury, usura, usurer*
threading two
-faced, spinning, un-
spinning, until he was spun.

Gold lay between the lines, amber & light,
the blossoms perfect
-ly light, air-

       less –

  in
tensely
  care-free –

In a poem he was later to write
I lay gold bricks across his body
one by one until he was buried
in bullion, covered in Monday.

Kneeling by his sweet light I prayed
I might come to love
to declare: *I don't hate, I love,*
I   l o v e –

Rising from my knees, I was dirty.
Words trickled in my throat
lala circling, spilling
the same rhythm, the same –

When I tried, when I began to speak,
to say, what to do? (*lala*)
unravel myth? (*lala*)

do?

Without his book I could not dream
his resurrection or recognize the blossom
not-yet-bloomed remained fragile & sweet.

He was, he boasted, all apple, both
fruit *and* seed, Father who stirred the branches,
flowering *in* things, *in* people, pushing
his way through. Relentless. Unyielding.

But, what did I know?

Only, that I'd been caught
only, if I shook the tree, shook it hard
I could shake its branches
loosen blossom, shake him.

But before I could shake, think, before –
he said I ought to creep about his tendrils. Quietly,
surely I obeyed. I crept. Surely
we kissed.

Trees blossomed, wind caressed
our cheeks, teased the moment, rose –
I did not like the image. There was dirt
on my hands & dress. My hair,
an ancient ruin.

It was torture this
bliss, his gold & delicious, made me
think of apples I might eat. One day.
He reminded me blossoms once bloomed,
fall faded to the ground.

I crept, we kissed & I pulled
fine twigs from my hair like bones
he was *in* things, *in* people.
My dress ruined.
My throat a trickle of *la*.

Reminding me of the brevity of spring
he read me William Morris quoting his own *Book
of Dreams*, his tendrils rooting
until he was earth & root & earth.

His words glittered brilliantly
in the sunlight, spinning, spun
I was his Greek goddess *(lala)* & he
my first kiss –

Enchanted, easily charmed –
Ah, yes,
yes, to answer your question, *yes* –
They must have been blossoms blossoming
in that apple-tree.
In that orchard.

RIGOR MORTIS

I had stopped
running. And he had stopped
to ask if I had ever kissed
a boy. I hadn't. He knew
& sought to show me how.

It was his word I wanted
mostly. Not warmth,
but magnetism. As I lay in the snow wanting
his breath, waiting –
It seemed significant, infinitely trivial
past feeling –

My first kiss, the winter woods stopped
running. I stopped to listen &
felt the slow cold lick of rigor mortis.
No longer feeling – I was cold, cold –

My coat soaked my skin hot,
I looked past the trees & the powdered snow
& dared to
stop.

Shadows fell upon the snow
like the Rock of Gibraltar I couldn't move
or remember the colour of his eyes, green
as pine needles, aren't they?

For a long while I lay in the snow wanting
his word. It was impossibly cold.

He wore a cap, he didn't.
I was impatient & quivered
as he pushed back shadows
our breath mingled & I felt
the slow cold lick of rigor mortis –

A VERY BIG FISH

There was something about his talk.
The way he could hold hands
with a ticking clock and make it love him.

(tic-talk-tic) *tic* –
He often missed
his train –

& the last whistle whistling his wants
into the pond. THUNK

He was a big fish,
swimming in & out & in
where many minnows tangled among the weeds.

His ideas, hooked & wormed,
& worm, so very ugly,
worm so very big, wiggled its way
along the bottom, free
of hook; it frightened the tiny fishes
his nakedness –

Numbers don't lie.
There weren't as many fish
in the pond as there had been.
Before.

Ah, he said, *the pond is holy.*
Ah, I said.

Afterwards, swimming, feet flapping
underwater I found no evidence
no lilies' sweet blooms blooming
in his pond.

He was a big fish, very
big & there were many minnows
swimming about the muck –

Ah, I said,
the needle pricking my arm –

Ah, he said,
What took so long?

THESE ROSES, THOSE THORNS

Ask for anything:
trips to Europe,
a grand piano,
Walter Morse Rummel.

Even now I will not trade
those roses half-bloomed for these
needling their way through a reluctant heart.
A rose is a rose too –

We read in the dark at the British Museum.
Everyone enjoying the gloom
& he, stalking the aisles, a lynx
among statues, slashing his quill pen.

Merciless, he batted my poems
between his great paws, shortening the lines
he pad-padded about, poured tepid
tea & agreed *Hermes of the Ways* a good fit.

There was blood on the floor where
I'd struggled writing the dark & gloom.
Poems curled their lines, lingered,
in the margins of the page, breathless
began to cross, uncross their long limbs
& kicking hard under the table, bruised my knee
& declared themselves roses about to bloom –

I ran towards his perfection. Inchoate &
awkward he took my trembling hand & signed
my name at the bottom of the page. It was dark.
& enjoying the gloom, I settled
in my chair, the room smelling of roses
& blood
& tea
& roses
about to bloom.

The hunt over; the kill complete;
limping towards perfection, padding
about the room, thorns in her thumbs
Hermes crawling on all fours –

That was the last I saw of Hilda.

YOU SPOKE OF GRAPES

In my friend's house
there are many rooms
with doors that open & close
& open.

I don't want to explain the intricacies
of biology, or elucidate pathological
impulses, equations. I've never had
a head for algebra. I failed, was
a failure, you remember
my failing?

Yet I was not jealous.
How could I be?

He was a Satyr.
Everyone knew it
& I, just a girl he carried
into the forest, even then
he did not complete the metamorphosis.

Padding through the woods tenacious, wild,
his flowering rod a shrieking mandrake knew
no bounds. Trees shook
& the forest, it seemed, submitted
to his whim. This was no Gothic illusion.

He was *Gawd's own God-damn country.*

His mandrake adrift in leaves, in the sound
of their rushing free, I suffocated.
I was TREE.

Shaken. I shook in my friend's house.
But even then, even then,
walls would not fall.

Doors opened. I was the one –
(he opened)
& suffocating
(he opened)

I was not jealous,
How could I be?

There was no naming this queer
quiver, this pulse,
& the mandrake shrieking
rooted in tree –

Here, where even the walls do not fall.
Trees shook, leaves rushed to escape the harlequin.
I was TREE –
Shaking, quivering –

But you spoke of grapes &
air & grapes &
suffocated,
I am starving –

II

Resisting Analysis

SMUDGED; I AM LOVE

There was no one to answer
but air, rather cool, tossed back her head
& laughed. My hair blew frantically when she pushed
& pulled, both; I didn't understand.

Was I to move
forward? Return
the way I'd come?
or remain standing,

stooped, the weight of the world mine
& the universe flashing gloriously
green & quick – time slowed, stopped, sped up,
a curtain of hair & wind.

Browning's cruel Duke boasting
rum & Coca-Cola, my glass & his hand,
anticipating Frà Pandolf
painting; my spot of joy,

half-flushed, cocked; compare this
to a summer's day. Its throbbing pulse,
its steady tremble, daylight to dusk.
Adjust the angle of their hats, just so

peaches hung firm & ripe in the orchard,
withered in the orchard; I was of two minds,
two separate worlds; fact & fiction,
watching the old man serve drinks reading

my future between well-thumbed pages,
the darkened words of D.H. Lawrence.
The arc of his hands rising above
his head: a rainbow, Neptune's seahorse

writhes under his rein; tugs, flies –
streams of colour, shades of green breath,
trees & leaves bloom, fade; what
did he say?

Stirring my drink, fact & fiction grow
quickly, suddenly, my fear of drowning;
Freud's train pulls into the station.

Choking, I swallow light, whole
& holy too between shadows knowing
myself alone on the train & the man
who speckles the wings of a passing pigeon,

skips a stone across a lake's surface,
rises from its watery grave, alive,
again, briefly, before rain, during
rain, the sky splits into cloud & gaze,

a sliver – daylight; a spirit weaves in
& out of the carriage. Again, my cheek
wets the window, spots; no one
to ask, to answer.

Am I to remain standing?

Stooped, I have never been uncertain
like this, smudged; I am love,
you are as well. Like the Professor,
his brush sweeping

against my forearm.
Ah my darling, you are here,
& the air cooler than it was before, when
she tossed back her head & laughed.

She tossed back her head & laughed.

See, the moon glows through the wreck
God's finger pointing, *here* –

Trees rise brilliant
in this holy light, bones turn

leaves & spin the seasons –
Winter, summer, ghosts

complain: *where did the earth go?*

Oh, I don't know,
I've stopped listening. Long

ago. Long ago Wind ran
out of breath, & impatient

with the World closed its sad eyes,
black spots on the sun.

Oh, I don't know!
if the poet spinning her spinning wheel

threads dreams; no one wants
her incantations. Who

feels so inclined to say, *what
comes first?* Night, anger, desire?

      What?
Words rattle loose

Bran's Sparrow, shut in a box
longs for a pen, a match, a small blue

flame. *What comes first?*
Oh, I don't know, fire or flame.

Laughing, sensing her hesitation,
I dropped a tooth in the grass. Wild

boar, walrus tusk, cat's eye. Some
antiquity stuck in the folds of Fortuna's skirt.

Dante's pricked rose stung the silver stem,
Apollo's sword: humility, glory –

What does it matter how
it spins? We climb;

we fall again.

Oh, what did I know of fire, or flame?
What do I know of ash?

Or unholy light & spinning bones
ecliptic, Milky Way ghosts –

MAGNOLIA

Without prayer the wheel stopped spinning.
My tea cold, my cup without its handle.
With nothing left to hold, faith grew
another mantra. Hope crossed
her legs, opened them & pressing the souls
of her feet together, tried to remember

the firm feel of flesh. Afterwards, she admitted
nothing came of it; & padding softly across the carpet,
was careful where she tread. Light strained the stillness:
morning, afternoon, lilies wilt in their vase.
Smell them, I implored. They had no sweetness
& heads bowed before the mirror, spotted

the inside of my wrists, brushed their marbled skin.
Yes, I knew joy, once, briefly, watching Medusa's mayhem
slither across the floor; scars I didn't wish disturbed
crawled back into bed. Copulating lovers didn't want
me. Who would?
A third wheel with cold feet & sharp nails.

Screaming her name: *Everyone,* she, her, someone
I used to know. *No one* – I will not repeat the name, or care
    enough
to say: *I love* – leave its dangling branches to sweep
four baby skunks, a lion cub, a young tygress, & lines of rats
scuttling from a crack in the ceiling. *What card is this? Who's*

playing? Ants fill the window ledge; I do not understand
this rain, fur, buzz of insect talk. I do not always understand
I'm getting wet, wanting sleep. Claws scrape
hieroglyphics, a hematic tale, quiet
voices argue; *what?* Plague ends
or begins in the lungs. The mouth gasps;

it's what you don't say. Make a clean sweep –
three of us, throats swelling, hands clenching.
Lambs? Magnolia? A fan spins
on the ceiling: *It is too hot.* The ring on my third
finger reeks of feces. Shat upon, out of house & home

the room fills with noise. Again
I'm itching, soiling sheets, sweeping,
the shape of his body bending towards her. From behind
he looks a satyr, wild, quaking; the room erupts,
where animals go to die. *Bleed babes; bleed slaughtered
lambs* – the piper & his Phrygian chant out of tune.

A sign, surely I would recognize configurations, recall
his voice, emulate joy, the shape of it moving. Hers,
mine, gyrating, the three of us, all at once;
my mouth foams, the wheel spins, I cannot speak,

Magnolia –

WHO BUT THE DEAD?

A black bear shimmies up a Harris pine,
rounds its back, hedgehog prickly, & perforates time.

My hand, lost in the pocket of my old coat,
curls around an acorn.

Wind in the oak leaves, *ah now* –
another day, another dusk.

Here we might live forever
mouth to mouth, say nothing, tell me nothing –

The sun shifts, sinks against the sky.
Still you do not wake; still

you do not stir. Rubbing the acorn
a week, a month, years pass.

Who but the dead measure time?

A back moon, Mercury retrograde.
I could dream, but it's crowded there.

Pictures, words; too many images
to decipher. I don't understand.

What happened yesterday? Before;
I was waiting for tomorrow,

Ah now –
I am listening for the dead.

Today tick-talks. The clock sighing,
will not rewind. September

ends without much to say.
Listen, that's the last strain of summer.

The cicadas do not sing
as loudly as they did before.
Squirrels jump from branch to branch,
leap from the vines, land on the roof

thump, thump –

Mother says it's raccoons;
I know better. *Look –*

There are apples, small ones,
gifts in the grass.

Dog is delighted & watches the sky
for falling fruit. The linden tree leans

against its branches. We are tired,
the sun sleepy, me too –

Rubbing the acorn I am perfectly content
thumbs pricking to think of you.

Reading late, playing fire
& light. Strike a match;

is it dark yet?

There are no stars in the sky.
Tygers, lambs, chimney sweeps,

a forest of bears disappears.
Innocence gone, a hedgehog loses all sense

of direction. Head full, fruit forgotten
in the grass, light fades. I do not recall

the hour. The last strain of summer;
A field of falling acorns. Wind

in the oak leaves. *Ah now –*

I fear the cicadas do not sing as they did before.

III

What Slender Birds

REFUSING PERSEPHONE'S BOWL OF FRUIT

Goodbye Dave,
you'll come over Christmas Day,
won't you?

That was the first I heard of him,
a tickle in my head calling names.
He didn't know mine;
he hadn't named me yet.

Perhaps the child's presence helped loosen
that slim line connecting me to him,
that long-ago-knotted thread,
slackened now, but always present.

I surprised myself by daring
to cross that rope, by refusing Persephone's bowl of fruit.
Instead, I cast myself to sea:
a garden of violets, winter rose, black crocus, lilies –
their long necks, their delicate heads still
standing after a wind-storm.

In the orchard, Botticelli nudes, we reach
for an apple, stretch
beyond the fruit, beyond,
the serpent flicking his forked tongue.

Ray slipped a rope around my neck.
Enticed by his promise of green,
& apples in the orchard,
& green; I joined him.
His firm flesh, his white lie.

He called me Queen of Love.
But never Aphrodite.

His release (from St Elizabeth's?)

Hopeless.

Mine? It lived in the *Cantos.*
Flicked its tongue in the tepid pools of September
where he sat fanning his angry flame,
threading his rope, offering fruit,
remembering green.

I could go either way:
to sea, or to the gates of St Elizabeth.

It was Easter Sunday.
His lovely voice spread before us larger than life
& wormed its way through our skin.

Are there apples yet on the tree?

The tickle tickled my throat,
the breeze in the blind,
shook, & curved my line of vision.
Yofi, licking my sweating palm
brought me back suddenly to the room
where light falls between afternoon & dinner,
black, grey; hours without a hint of green.

It was Easter
& thinking of his resurrection –
the snake in the garden flicked its forked tongue,
nudes, fat from eating apples, sick
from eating apples, knew to leave worm alone.

& the rope?

A thin thread about my finger.
I could snap it with my teeth.

His prison, where lines held the page, stark & black.
Ray's image without a trace of green,
without a hint of salt or blossom –
took my breath. Suffocated, drowned
I was afraid, still –
he called me Queen of Love,

but never Aphrodite.

Maybe I care when the needle pricks my arm
to remember the garden, or how he might have seemed
surrounded by the minnows May called *her* poets.

& the water cold, too cold
pulling the arm of the needle –
the story mid-way, that could not, would not,
conclude.

Which shore to cross, which shadow?
My shoulder, aching for the weight
of Balzac's androgyny, its pedantic simplicity,
its image of air.

Ezra in the garden
ins rechte Licht

Séraphitus died in the snow
where we first kissed
the perfection of that moment –
the soft imprint of our bodies where
I lay to receive him.

My head, God's thumb-print?
The same. Once
touched. I was tired –

Drawing the needle,
May, her hair still in curl-papers,
stood unashamed by our sudden appearance,
a statue welcoming the light. Even then I knew
this fiery moment too rare, too bright;
I would not look directly –

Her shoulders, bare, shone,
each tress of hair bound, forever curled
& lovely. As if set in
marble, the moment chiseled memory,
stone.

He asked why I didn't look at him, why
I didn't want to talk.
I answered:
Shadows are disturbed by the heaviness of words.

His limbs, fins as he swam
among the minnows, circled:
once, twice, a third time.
May in her curl-papers, stood
 a statue, her arms stretched around the sun
caught its glow. It was only a moment;
I did not follow his gaze.

The needle pricked, (I had forgotten its prick) –
but I did not forget the light, silver & brilliant,
or May standing like a goddess welcoming us
at such an early hour, or the minnows swimming
round the big fish anxiously flipping their fins.
One look from him, & Jesus
walked on water. Veins pulsed

in my head. My eyes watered in that holy light
Ray dove beneath the surface, his breath
bubbling. Fishes scattered in every direction.
Tiny ripples on a tiny pond.

I stood where there were no shadows.
Unsure which shore to cross,
my head heavy, my lungs, aching for air –

GIVEN TO UNNATURAL LUST

Then, I did not understand;
I did not know that word.

It was 1906, '07
& we did not speak of it.

There were signs of course: William's grief,
his consumptive sister's grave miles from the cemetery
& the letter he wrote – the flowered hand
Ray would not let me touch.

There were eccentricities (some overlooked):
bright lurid socks,
cousin Ed's talk,
a woman bedded in the snow,
Ray's frequent trips to the lily pond.

Before & during I was reading *A Lume Spento*
& coming to the 15ème jour lunaire, I stopped
praying & rose from my knees to talk
with Mary, Bessie & Louise.

Father requested Ray not visit so very
often any more. There would be no
announcement, no party where
I might fling my glass to the floor
& shatter any implication
we would wed –

There was little hope now.

It was 1906, '07 & I did not know
the meaning of that word, but I knew
town gossip, & the fiery kisses
I'd so readily given had been so
readily received.

There were signs, of course:
He wore brilliant socks
& visiting the lily pond
bedded a girl in the winter snow,
returned her broken that spring –
Common knowledge to everyone, to
Mary, Bessie & Louise, but not,
not to me.

I did not know the meaning,
that word, & its perpetual sting
had yet to be invented:
Oedipus complex,
inferiority complex,
claustrophobia.
Agoraphobia.

The list was necessarily long.

I couldn't equate or imagine such possibilities:
this,
that, this
again & …

Yes, of course, of course,
(how very German of you for asking)
I did return the ring –

But I kept the pearls.
I kept his mother's pearls –

Was that wrong of me?

There were two red roses strung across the moon.
Guinevere, busy, defended herself against thorns
& roses, blackened her eye, scratched, half-closed, almost –

I wanted to quote a passage from *King Lear*
madness I had forgotten. The moon appeared
quite suddenly in quarters. *Snip*
snip. It was neatly done.

Then, there were only the three of us.

At ten o'clock he brought me into the house where
he had written another sonnet bound in parchment,
sowed the orchard thick with gadflies.

Someone had written a novel, someone
was climbing Mt Olympus?
A wingless horse fell from the sky,
its horseman flew unsure
if he was landing hooves up or down
his nose pointed to heaven, or hell?
Horse or man? It was all so sudden. Either
interpretation would do.
It mattered;
I think.

What happened to the horse?

He kept flying, or trying to.
His wings weren't wax. & the moon, her face covered
in roses, her lovely face pricked by thorns,
no longer seemed very pretty.

Just the two of us
& the air so thick with gadflies
it was impossible to separate the dead
who began to wind honey, suckle on nuts,
chimed the house clock, *ten, ten.*

Repeating its dull message; I was sick
of hearing, tired of listening.
Snipsnipsnip

It had taken too long to remember
the author; *who rode the horse, who
was its rider?* It was Ray always,
& air thick with gadflies.

Who spoke of Swedenborg?
William Blake?

God, poets, ghosts.
There were lambs, tygers burning
in the orchard. The arrangement was
harmonious.

I did not complain when he
called me Is-hilda. I pretended
not to hear. In another story his wings
are fire, falling leaves. When he whistles
for a dragonfly, apples ripen. In August he is bitten
on the ass …
(is there any other way?)

This arrangement too was harmonious.

At eleven o'clock I followed him into the house
bound in parchment, I could not move.
Another winged sonnet stung the horse's head.

The King had momentarily forgotten
Guinevere. Too busy defending herself
from roses & thorns, she had forgotten him.
Later there were apologies. Everyone
so sorry – *sorry* –
Then the three of us:
he & I & the orchard moon
snipped –

& the air, the air, so very
thick with gadflies –

SIPPING A GLASS OF CHIANTI

I have seen the lion restless
in its cage pad-pawing above my bed
banging its head violently, uselessly,
against its frame, against its bars.
There could be no escape.

Now, sipping a glass of Chianti I notice
there are birds, a Minotaur, more birds
& still the lion does not growl, & still –

The world's a sham I think
in my black lace cap my belly swollen with child
I'm no sylph & he, no Minotaur,
but a lion banging its head, pounding
as if he's pacing the tick
of the clock, my confinement
perfectly timed. Even then,
Maestro conducts our lives
as he would have them.

Too sick to scream or beat his baton
against the wall; I was too ill to care.
Time's steady thump – my expanding belly,
the child coming, almost,
not yet –

His baton sagged in the middle;
his rhythm was not what it had been,
before –

Even in my stupor I knew
the lion was not a Minotaur;
its roar did not overwhelm
the redness of the wine, its all-
colour –
nothingness.

My glass was full, his?
Too readily consumed
less than halfway to the rim.

He had taken
what can I say? –
a name, what is that?
The disappearing do-little.
Never missed or wanted –

Pounding rhythmically,
his stick, struck hard, this way,
that – O,
I was too ill to care what I had
done & had no regrets. Too late
for sorry, for that – my glass half-full,
his drained –

I am not saying,
I did not see the Minotaur.
Or feel each blow –

The cage shook
(I was too sick to care). Rattled
above by head & the child almost come.
There could be no escape.

Even in my stupor, I knew
the lion was not a Minotaur
& the birds, too many to name
would soon take flight & disappear.

SO MANY FISHES, SO MANY LOAVES
OF BREAD

It was April when he took my hands
& placing them between his asked,
May I?
But I had no answer.
Harvest seemed a long way off.

Dreaming of fishes &
small loaves of bread
there were no fishes;
there were no loaves of bread
only apples heavy on a bough
small pockets, indentations pressing
air. I thought only I could see,
only I could tell their season, &
I didn't want to.

Returning to the orchard I dipped my hands
into air's soft dimples and did not see
the light change, or the apples spinning on their stems,
or how his hair seared the sky & left
it burning. Feeling
the heat, a lick of flames he spoke,
Bless me, Saint Hilda, bless me.
My face flushing madly, briefly –

He was busy, *so very busy* living
as a troubadour might, celebrating
love & all its conventions, making unreasonable
demands I wasn't always sure
were unreasonable.

I might have placed my hands upon his forehead
& smoothing its lines, cooled his fever, mine.
But I didn't want to.
I was through smoothing.
Already his mouth had smudged my face
with kisses, sweet. I took them (sweet
sweet), not noticing he had also taken
my head & replaced it with another.

Stilled by his flame. Like the rest, all
of us, awed by his fervour, temporarily –

What did it matter?
There were volumes of love.
I had only to find myself,
Dryad among the ruins to re-member my robes,
my long long bones stretched a thousand fold.
I grew taller, much.
& touching heaven I held
hands with the gods.

Odysseus called to him & disappearing
behind a bushel of apples,
Ray latched the swinging gate.

Pomona. Pomona. Christo Re, Dio Sole.

As if a wave hit.
As if,
as if –

The momentum gone, the rhythm altered.

People are things, things people.
People are *in* names, names *in* people –
But I found none of us there.

The gate locked, the epic continued.
Lines flooded the page.
There was no getting in,
or out. I could not walk on water;
I could not balance
what was real from what he imagined
& commanded to be so.

Another wave, I slipped on sea-foam,
white caps; I swam from the *Cantos*
but made no headway. I had no head –
Half-flushed,
breathless, I muttered,
Bless you –

& I might have meant it, if
I'd wanted to.

Then, before
then, there were so many fishes,
so many loaves of bread –

ITS OWN TROUBADOUR

How you weave over & back,
he said without meaning.
I had stopped

listening. Reading the *Cantos*, I had taken
on too much. The images were daunting,
& dazed, I was dizzy with remembrance
tripping on the rug, the war, the Blitz
blitzing & she
killed –

The book had a mind of its own
& wanting love among the troubadours,
was its own troubadour – its own beloved.
It spoke a darling French.

I was its only Lady. A saint so filled
with roses I was both blossom
& thorn. Stiff from praying,
I could not stand, or dream, or look
past the long line of trees in the orchard.
I could not see his sun;
I could not see that far.

Among the dryads day felt a little thin.
Pages yellowed, strings unbound
troubadours, who voiceless, could not sing
of love, & the poet, I was convinced, was infatuated
with himself. Neither held
relevant meaning. Too many long agos,

too many ifs – I was reading the *Cantos* & found it too much
the language of young love.
Weaving the war, spooling its threads
I was all thumbs; I was having trouble with the dead
who wouldn't rest quietly;
who wouldn't stay still.

Don't say anything, he said.
His only criticism, then, the child wasn't his.
He had missed the point, almost
completely. Then

I was reading the *Cantos*. I had taken
on too much. The dead wouldn't lie still
& I was dizzy with remembrance, tripping
on troubadours, the rug, the war, the Blitz
& she killed.

The images were daunting;
the dryads thin as day, voiceless,
had no relevant meaning.
& I, I too could not sing.

IV

un-UNKing the UNK

NOT IN HER LOVELY

One jab would do it.
Back arcing, hands stretched taut;
I am floating & fish, gulping
air, etherized.

Pale pink scales shine, flicker
helplessly on the ceiling; fin & flap.
Words? I might have said
as the needle finds its nerve,

swims backwards, forwards, circles
about the spine. Funny, sort of a coincidence really,
a ring, a bangle snaring her dress, brushing
memory in the cloakroom, this strange light,

Katherine's last visit to Paris. Anything is
possible. Walk on the promenade? A man,
a woman, sit upon a bench. Patient before
the window, her velvet frock, a soft blue

good-bye, good-bye – But you don't mean it.
Smell the smoke, charred flesh, frazzled
hope; it drifts to sea. She, no, not in her lovely
blue – waves, wildly, softly, signal fading.

Now we are both lost, drifting. Out
of our element. Coughing wakes me.
Hers, mine. *Listen, I see spots.* Time
has no recollection. It, she, I can't

remember the orange glow. Katherine's cigarette
as it fluffs her small features from pea to
poppycock – shaking her stick, denying her
presence, the ticking clock, its glorious hum,

her pen scratching. *Ah that* – Anything is
possible; I might write across the page, the nib draws ink
in a jar, stains her bandages. Pretty phrases, *a fine review.*
Unaccustomed to blotting, I smudge what I have

written. Katherine isn't impressed. Not easily. Two people
rising, no longer sit upon the bench. The Promenade waves
goodbye; goodbye, you don't mean it. Waves lap; my fins
flap uncontrollably; the room grows larger where

she paces. Holes grow in the carpet. Pink threads, pale,
this strange light; I might follow their pattern. A bow draws
across a cello string. Hers? Does it matter? Love strains
for its tug, the needle pricks; music stops as if

it doesn't belong. He, she, remembers, nonetheless.
Listen, *I am D.* I am sleeping. Parched & late
for an appointment. The doctor asks,
You all right? Water burns my cheeks. A bow presses

across my throat. Snapping unexpectedly, it hurts.
I hurt like hell. The cello? He asks. *Yes, yes.*
I am repeating myself. *Well, that's to be
expected,* he says. It's funny, a coincidence

really, the bench, its lovely
blue fin flapping, signals cross;
we are lost,

each of us, drifting –

I held out my hands. A bowl
with nothing in them.
Refusing my offer, she began
to laugh. I wasn't sure

I heard, or if imagined,
I gave her smile more meaning
than desired. Remembering Sappho
& the sisters, I wondered

who spoke: she, I, who
came before?
Shimmering in the light, her face
came into focus. Holy & human, she rose
a full moon in the morning,
each blessed spot a nestling.
Lacking patience, unable to sit

still, I worship from afar, inept;
unrecognizable. How
could I know? My begging
hands, my stooped shoulders –

The weight of this world, & the next
bends like a wish-bone
-wished already broken
beyond hope –

My bowl empty, fuller
than it was, before,
What,
must I beg?

Again, she is laughing,
when I hold out my hands
the idea fills me –

Catching the emerald she threw
stones of light, twigs, griffin feathers
fluttered in the green; I reached
towards them, turning

Time's screw
& slowed it –
You are a proper idiot,
she says, her face shining.

We continue playing, she & I,
Hermes & Aphrodite, stoic,
tossing the stone,

the jewel so near my grasp air rushes
between the spaces of my fingers,
I knew it might

unknot the underworld;
grip the holy
grail, & like that, just –

I was filled with longing –

AMONG THE RUINS

I.

If I'd been wearing shoes, then yes,
I would have made my way past
crumbling plaster & ceiling wax, broken
nails, floor boards, sitting slant –

Fearless, I might have tread upon thread-bare
carpet, known its stories stained in wool; the light
unrelenting, now forgotten, forgave
my distraction. Indiscretions at the window:

the petite shadow of forget-me-nots lean their tender
bodies, purple & bruised against the head of thistle
& there, grow enormous. Exhausted,
an old woman squints into morning, holds her breath,

spreads her hand like a sparrow's wing, *Home* she calls it,
tracing the gentle curve of sky, the slope of his shoulders,
    Keats
crouching in the unkempt grass. Pants down waiting
for Spring, he leaps toward Summer too soon –

I could hear her shudder, wind tugging her skirts. Pools
    rippled.
Ponds don't lie. Neither poet nor I was ready;
such rains we knew, require puddle-jumping,
mad leaps of faith, brilliant thick-soled boots.

Pebbles ribbed the shore, reluctant
leaves slung between branches. I might have run
towards them, thrown stones at the breeze & declared
the season turned. The woman before

the window ruffled her feathers & waving this uncertain
quiet, parted rain's long hair, unravelled July
so that worm wiggling, sank in the earth,
& the robin hungry, calling wildly, shrilly,

bid the fornicating poet,
which day is this?

II.

If I'd worn shoes sensible to nails or quivering
timbers would it have mattered if silt grew
along the river, or sunlight's shaft burned
the termites' holes to dust?

Grabbing air, the dead drown words.
What was said? Was said
before. Boldly, or not
I might have turned each room into an eye

looking for someone familiar, I knew.
The smell of breath, black & anxious for talk,
I found them Romantically inclined: lyric
iambic, both. Phrases peppered in uneven

pentameter; I stood among the ruins
barefoot, distrusting the feel of fall. I had every
intention of telling you I was not afraid –
Scorpions clung to the walls, the largest flicked

its orange tail & certain my heart would stop –
Its sting opened doors, morning, swollen & green
sounded in the field of the house, a siren's song buzzed

in my head. Humming Keats's stanza I sprung
to wake a Lady mourned among the dead. Hieroglyphics,
flashed. I had forgotten their peace,
images flew – it was raining? *Who*

or what is this, my sparrow?

Away from the window, light shines
on my feet, my white marbles. Antiquity –
Drained, I'm tired, so very
& the flood of drowning, & its dull green ache –

Who was watching, when
the wheels began to spin?

The road home?
Pockmarked. Sinkholes

the size of casserole dishes
bowls of soup, pots, pans –

I was hungry;
I had not eaten.

Dimes swam through cloud,
sea birds, flakes of snow.

Saucers without cups spinning
bread & butter plates,

but no bread & butter.
Not a crust, not a crumb

to spare & spent,
hunger consumed me.

There were no signs;
I did not know him.

Understand the palimpsest
had another page to write.

My head rattled
& sensibilities shaken

I did not resurrect
River grasping for breath.

Frantic, waves beat
Jachin & Boaz, bashed.

Beauty & Strength gone –

O shame
for not shifting

the moment forward
or back to safety

O shame –

I was tired,
hungry. Angels

did not share their feast.
Blood-blots on the surface

waves, water-marks. Stigmata
stains the sky.

Read: *Crumbs.*
Broken bread.

Freud's voice crackled over the line:

Stoppen
Stoppen

The recording looped back,
flowered five petals in its dark rose.

Blossom & thorn, both
bloomed in my hands.

For a moment, I held eternity
its bright promise, satiated,

At last –

O Shame

My brother found me
crumpled in the snow;

dimes, pentacles, scattered
among the angels. Falling

asleep dream of vineyards,
red wine, winding roads.

A labyrinth of crumbs.
& no way home.

Laughing, the angels disrupt
my sensibility.

Stoppen
Stoppen –

I am lost & fall
where the earth drops to water

waiting for the ferryman.
River wails:

I want to go home!
I am tired & hungry.

I am tired & hungry;
my old heart bends

a crust of bread,
waves. Another page.

Where wheels spin Winter to ice,
vision, no, nothing

ecstatic. Angels well fed
& fat; I know

are not for me.

BEAUTY MADE ME STRONGER

He was standing at the crossroads alone
& I was running by the forest, alone.

Together, he made me forget
myself & time. Was it morning?
Night? The afternoon brilliant,
& the moon unyielding.

I ought to be afraid,
but beauty made me stronger,
his, the moon, both; I had only
to make up my mind.

A slanted life,
borrowed memory,
another dream?

I couldn't decide.

Freud was scribbling notes, & Wolfsmann
on the couch, feared
his pack might soon pounce upon him –

I would have preferred weeping to silence.
A gesture, a word –
Lycanthropy, lycanthrope, lykos.

I didn't understand.
Fairy-tale, myth?
What did it matter?

I knew too much, not enough
about anything & nothing
to know wolf's message remained
unclear, but steady, omnipresent.

& the moon?
A clock ticking sticks on a moment then
ticks no more –

Placing Richard's wrist watch on her arm,
counting the hours between
war, no man's land, & endless cups of tea.

Search for a beginning, a start,
but re-membering thought of Diana
who slipped on air,
& skidded into wolf.

Then, I did not understand the brightness,
the loud rush, silence, wind's warning,
the breathtaking beauty – all of it.

Stumbling, the track slick, what
might they say? *Shame*
shame … like her sister … shame –

Later, the conductor recalled:
A wolf is
a wolf –

Not believing, translating air,
the rush of spring sprung.
No memory of life,
Saturn spun all angles:

hope, time, Haiti, Fenrir,
Freud's analysis & Wolfsmann's nightmare
mean nothing –

The mind plays tricks,
makes stories.
In the beginning voices spoke.

Join their chorus:
Lupa, Feronia –

My metamorphosis grew in trees,
wolf's nearly complete.
I ought to be afraid,
but beauty made me stronger –

V

Newsreels

HILDA IN THE ORCHARD

It could be Troy again if we let it.
But there was nothing more to sacrifice.
The Maestro, already under lock
& key was strangely silent.

Loyalties were divided.
God or man?
Motive or method?

Italy was his she-wolf,
Frobenius, his German father.
I was through battling egos.
Through with war. My Blitz long since
blitzed. Long since burned.

We lit candles for his birthday, praised his connection
to God, King & the troubadours wooing love.
For a moment I was Hilda in the orchard.
It was harvest; an explosion of fruit
& I was hit by apple.

Limbs spoiled, they no longer looked fresh
or flawless. The body once beautiful,
withered & sagged.
Fallen, I'd had enough of egos, war & blackouts
& lighting candles with one match.

Loyalties were divided. In the Beinecke Library
they spoke Italian, German & English.
I ought to have spoken Greek,
but instead sat still translating God
& King, & Ray, my head spinning,
spinny.

Fearing Moravian manners might betray me,
I said very little, & quoting the virtues of love
in the afternoon dared not
record truth, or tell,

what?

The gods, the critics, I think, grew angry.
We were not who or
what we seemed.

With nothing more to sacrifice,
the Maestro, already under lock
& key was strangely silent.
Loyalties were divided.
Bruised, I couldn't lift my arm,
my hand, my pen withdrew to the library
where it wrote only in Greek
& wasn't properly understood.

It might have been Troy again –
but I'd had enough of war,
& blackouts, & lighting the last match
to burn the last candle.

Fanning that flame, I found myself
crouching, afraid in the dark
I was not who or
what I seemed –

WOLF IS A WOLF

I did not understand his darkness,
Chthonian gloom, the howling wolf.

His metamorphosis nearly complete.
Mine? I could hardly walk. I had slipped
translating air, walking to Greece.

I did not recognize the myth then:
Peire Vidal, his love, Lady Loba,
troubadours & poets. Ray
& his warning of pigs.

I looked up the words:
Lycanthropy, lycanthrope, lykos.
Chamber's hinted at other connections:
feline, panther, lynx.

There were, I thought, certain omissions. Black
outs. My reluctance to shadow
his door. His shape
shifting. The image
gone –

When the moon was full, he wrote:
You have crawled into the sty.

True, I had been fast with pigs –
a little honey & wine I discovered
were mine as long as I wanted.
I did not want for long –

Understand I was,
I thought, the beginning.

The procession was lengthy. Maenads fed
his blood, mine, his love,
whose? Love

when it is so –
Together, we were more
apart than together,
before.

I did not understand his darkness
or hold his fennel staff –

Wolf by another name is wolf:
Dionysus, Bacchus. I looked for light
to guide me, for some sign, an acknowledgment
all was right, all was good,
but slipping on air,
translated my way again to Greece.

Without his troubadours or poets, Ray feasted
upon the dead. The procession was very long.
I had blackouts, lapses –

A wolf is
a wolf, I said.
Whispering in the dark,
I waited for the moment
translating air, stepping back, back –
my metamorphosis nearly complete.

HIS HEAD, A POMEGRANATE

Bushel baskets of beauty
scattered grains across the grass –

I was trying to understand,
to explain the photograph, his
hair: wheat-coloured, swath,
wound itself about a young girl & glued
her to his side.

Walking round & round with nowhere to go,
with nothing to do,
   ('round & 'round)
not minding, not a bit –
There was no exit to escape together.

She, me, that other self
sticky with adoration, knew
what I ought to know,
nothing else –

Father, burning Ray's letters,
sought to remove every trace.
I continued to believe love might blossom;
but it was hopeless to forget, or pretend
to resurrect the living & move about
lynx, Dryad, guardian of the gates.
I knew only what I ought to have known.

Immortal, gods among the Saints
we were young & terribly important,
our sultry lines floated blue & inky.
Master and Maestro, his traps set;
there would be no resurrection,
that much I knew;
that much I sensed –

In the dim halls of St Elizabeth, the light
narrowed, broadened, & reminded me of his hair
spreading across the grass, tawny & swath;
I could not follow its path; I could not
make sense of him.

Before the gates closed, his head was very like a
    pomegranate,
ripe & full of forgetting. But I had not forgotten.
How could I?
Keeper of the gates, I stood in the hushed halls of
    St Elizabeth
thoughts fluttering, a pink moth, lost
in the brilliance, flummoxed by the promise
of morning, the sun swelling shadow
against shadow, my wings beat
frantically against the light knowing
there was no exit, for me, him; among the Gods
we grew old.

Rereading the *Cantos,* I found fire
in his dark descriptions of fruit,
Maenad and Bassarid, my pink moth
crazed, fluttered staccato among his symphony,
chased his crazed stick –

Agèd, shrunk of flesh & bone,
I did not think it necessary
to explain the She, me, that other
self glued to his side who knew
what she ought to know:
nothing else –

I don't remember the ending, except
he was gone. Circling the cottage several times,
still he did not find what he was looking for.

Love? She had not forgotten
him. Making lists, she catalogued each time
he knocked upon her door. It hadn't been often,
that was the story; it didn't matter

what he said, or who he played
we waited for him to speak, attentive,
on the edge of our seats. We loved
him, or mostly –

He was, they said, King of the crazed.

I don't remember the rest.
But I remember watching Richard Mansfield's last
    performance
& how he held his hand over his liver &
prayed for sin.

Refusing to see the world as troll,
a woman in the audience raised her voice
above the flutes & yelled:
Jack, go home!

Where's that? Peer answered.

Heaven or hell? Ray added.

I was in love, or so I thought
imagining Mansfield's eyes upon me.
What did I know?

Ray was gone & circling about my father's house, once,
maybe twice more, concluded without warning;
he had not found what
he was looking for.

Holding my hand over my liver
just then, like Richard Mansfield (exactly so),
I prayed hard for sin & finding it oddly to my liking,
concluded I was not wife or wifely enough;
I was not at all what
he was looking for.

After the bombing, after
the after-time knowing
loss, I sensed darkness (not darkness)
– you, her,
& everything mattered.

Weightless, there was no ground
for grounding. The air walked
backwards, wherever that might be.

Lifting my skirt unbalanced my stand.
Not wishing to see or be seen,
I found her just as I'd left her: beautiful,
terribly young, but alive in the *Cantos*.

Tongues already wagged, yet
the Serpent refused to raise its head –

Le Paradis n'est pas
artificiel

Anyway, I had forgotten
I was intoxicated by Kuthera,
a thin trail of myrrh burning on a stick,
Hatshepsut's transplanted tree the same
far away, rootless, clinging to nothing –
nothing mattered –

Bombs,
the world breaking:
(pebbles
agony
pebbles) –

& no longer seeing wholeness, I sensed
darkness & squinted hoping to see
Penelope lean into the shadows
& step through narrow bars of light.

But the weight was too great,
or the space too small to pass through easily, &
stooped, she became an old woman, a shrew
shaking useless bars, her frail arms bending
two v's, two birds, seagulls that would not,
could not fly –

Now the picture whirls, the kaleidoscope
spins:
Erebus, no
Paradise –

O agony,
his uneven lines smoothed
my constant rub, made imprints,
tiny pebbles against my palms. Pockets.
Remembered.
Story.
Whose story?

Reading Benet's *Encyclopedia* searching
for an image among the ruins,
I found Leucothea, white foam,
a seagull soaring. She pitied Odysseus.
I pitied her. Neither of us recognized
Penelope desperate for the post.

Like them I couldn't find clarity;
words blurred
(my eyes closed)
crazy crazy
Indented palms suggested
lives stopped, started, stilled.
Reincarnation.
Restoration.
But I did not feel rested, or renewed.
Perhaps, I did not feel –

Slipping between this word & that.
The myth disappeared in an instant –
I rubbed small stones between my hands,
disturbed ghosts. All
that might have been.
If – Yes,

he was insane, always,
we knew it. Then.

I was war, unsettled,
jagged around the edges too
broken to break cleanly
into She or He,
Imagist or Hilda.
Lover or loved.
Perhaps I did not feel –

There are pebbles yet in my pockets
Small ifs –

Perhaps we were both too broken
to break cleanly, or come when called by name
floating & floated, landless,
the air sank & stirred beneath my feet.
Everything mattered too much,
too much, not enough –

The Serpent rose, lifted its head as if
to remember: water, motion,
the depth of long ago parted seas.

For one beautiful moment
the world was holy
& the Dark too thick for shadows –

Terrified, I screamed for Penelope,
whom I knew to be drowned.

We were all, I think,
a little crazed. He was of course
undone, perfectly,

insanely
mad –

THE MYTH CAN NOT BE LOCALIZED

I felt the grit of premonition:
an Ogre scuffling past the gate
dragged himself through Pisan, Rock-Drill, Lotus Land.

Radio Rome was playing, the frequency breaking
in/out
& most of us long gone home.

Yet I could not say with certainty
he walked alone, or if
she walked beside him, but

my whole creative output, volcano &
crystal, centred on those two.
I could not see either clearly.

Outside, the train rumbled
five five five days before I *must* imagine
the doors closing behind him at St Elizabeth's
& the wolf reappearing, shaking its prey,
snapping its neck.

The Ogre it seemed would live again.

Yet it would be the last time
we spoke. Illness, delirium, madness –
Why wait for the old Poet,
the Faithful wife, tolling bells?
Why wait?
It was all there in the *Cantos*
or mostly.

Hysterical, I could not cry.
Radio Rome was playing loudly when
I held out my hand & shifted
the present to steady the vison.

Static shook & my ears remembered
its unsteady pitch.
Ogre could not, would not
be stopped.

Turning, the last shimmer,
the glistening tracks,
the train whistles, brightly:
who who
who's next?

We were just
as he'd left us; restless,
fighting the same clichés, devil & doll
& he swinging cudgels, all air
& no heft.

The vision fading, I did not recognize
the changing light, or the stuttering train that filled
the room with sound where he lay on his belly
writing the *Pisan Cantos*. Our names appear one by one
bones he sniffs, rattles into impossibly, impossible verse.
Slanted words, sideway meanings –

The wolf must eat;
he will have us –

I was hysterical. Tears prevented me from crying
the bell's toll, the train's whistle,
the radio's sputtering stutter.

The myth we knew could not be localized.

It was there in the *Cantos*,
or mostly –

Its silent sputter rode past my ears,
spit volcanic eruptions burning,
blistered my skin.

I was afraid, wolf or Ogre,
what did it matter?

Everyone else long gone
Everyone else –

Alone,
I was afraid –

VI

Conversing with the Dead

CONVERSING WITH THE DEAD

Asleep, its rattle curved like a babe's thumb; I wasn't afraid
the serpent might wake, or if the sistrum, shaken
had already dispelled the dead. A stranger
in a strange place, I didn't know
this silent night where no bells rang.

Mouth stiffening, each letter needed proper annunciation.
Who would hear me speak? Alone
what did it matter what I said?
Hathor, who hears my echo, mocks me, finds me

wanting, dares me raise my stick. I poke about
the snake's head, jab its eye, but it remains
closed. The breeze stops, time displaced,
stumbles into character, a B western
on the wrong side of a deserted town. Sinking

into a falling sky, I haven't the strength required
to settle the sun or tuck her in
beside the two of us, sleeping – I couldn't decide:
if I'd written the day's end, dizzy, anticipating grief:
today, tomorrow, I grow weary drawing conclusions.

Time pauses: day, then night, the film flickering
cracks down the middle. Dust rises from the points
of my cowboy boots, stars where seasons come & go.
Opening my mouth I eat another sandstorm & drift
back to sleep, certain I will rouse the serpent, sistrum

shaking, ask cacti to blossom in my cheek. Pricked
& flowered, resurrected, I lift my leg
over the snake's sleeping body, but fail to find its ghost.
In another story, the serpent slayed, hangs above my head,
a crown of blazing glory, a thread threading cloud,
   constellations,

an exit from this labyrinth, this night's eye, unveils Hades,
   a world
of restless dead. *Look*, one limps behind another;
the wind rises to remind me *there is breath*, life;
the universe dare not disturb the snake struggling
to escape analysis, all is forgotten –

Why do gods hold my tongue, shake it, an old rug, beaten –
I'm worn through & through, the dead tell me,
I've said too much. Mythologies coil in the grass: earth & weed.
Cacti bloom. The sun no longer drops
hints & warns sparrows it's almost time

to sing of mourning. Whitman, pale
& mauve, wanders still longing
for forbidden fruit & 24 hour supermarkets.
I didn't see him but sensed his presence,
smelled his wild scent.

Lilacs in his arms were thick with blossom, heavy
with spring, & bent, the old man, wishing
apples in my cheeks might, heart might, fill
with wonder & awe. He was careful to shape his mouth
as he spoke each word. Just so –

He blew the perfect *O* in menthol smoke about his head. Halos,
replicas, the same cool question I was writing
signing my name in the earth, scraping
hieroglyphics trying to remember & be

re-membered. The tip of my cowboy boot, fumbled:
God Bless America, resisting analysis

conversing with the dead –

It was supposed to be spring
when I saw the griffon, yet
his wings full of snow, sagged with the weight
of winter, & his beak, caked in ice
froze the daily news solid
between his chops. April
would remain, April.

Wednesday would be that Wednesday
blossoms would not bloom.
The war continued. You could hear bullets
rushing through wind. The griffon,
starved, took a bite of apple I was eating
& lit the sky red.

Then the world on fire; I wanted
to return to winter, to that bird &
its cold news, but instead
reclining on the couch, my hands dangling
over the furniture I stirred the flames,
of desire; I stroked plumes of smoke.

Yofi came trotting into the room
& licked my salty palms. First one, then
the other, then a look from Rex
sent him to his master's side.

Afterwards, I drank white wine from the Holy Grail
& ate apples at the Wien and der Wein.
I sat outside crying for lilacs &
was embarrassed for myself.
There was blood on my pillow.
It was August, & the sun high
on light & air turned the myth I was dreaming.
Again it was spring,
wasn't it?

Fido's Paw-pat thumped miles away;
his whiskers flickered with light, his fur jumped
with fleas & his paws frantically scratching
air, an impossible itch, itched.
It was an impossible war,
a lovely dog –

I believed I could burn that burning
candle by the bed & the dream, bruising
the skin beneath my eye purple & sleepless,
winter circled above. It was dark –
I don't remember –

Dangling my hands over the rim
my wine glass hummed as I swallowed
a bite of apple. Sirens sang
in the streets, yet I did not move
to join them, instead bowed my head
to griffon's frantic thrashing.

Beating the air senseless,
the war might have ended
on that last hit,
on that flat note –

There was blood on my pillow.
When I woke someone had lit
the candle by my bed. I could smell
wax and imagined a puff of smoke
swimming towards light.

The myth turned.

Lilacs reluctant to open stood against
the light, stoned the sun to sleep opening
their eyes, branches punched air.
The winter gone, the ice broken
& the war? –

The griffon held the daily news,
frozen between its chops.
It was winter; it was cold.
A spot of blood stained my pillow.

NOTES

While it must be said that all of H.D.'s texts inspired this book, the following works were most instrumental: *End to Torment* (*ETT*) (New York: New Directions, 1979), *Tribute to Freud* (*TTF*) (New York: New Directions, 2012), *Bid Me to Live* (*BMTL*) (New York: Dial, 1960), *HERmione* (*H*) (New York: New Directions, 1981), *Notes on Thought and Vision* (*NOTAV*) (London: Peter Owen, 1988), *Magic Mirror* (*MM*) (Victoria, BC: ELS Editions, 2012), and Susan Stanford Friedman, ed., *Analyzing Freud: The Letters of H.D., Bryher, and Their Circle* (*AF*) (New York: New Directions, 2002).

"Fiery Moments": "The perfection of the fiery moment can not be sustained – or can it?" (*ETT* 11) Later in her diary entry H.D. admits, "I can not explain to him [Dr Heydt] how painful it is to me at times to retain the memory of the 'fiery moment'" (*ETT* 24). A child reaching into a market basket is the "fiery moment incarnate" (*ETT* 33).

"Last Train to Wyncote": H.D. and Pound escape to their favourite maple tree and crow's nest where they can hear the trolleys passing. H.D. wants to remain forever in the treehouse, but Pound reminds her it is the last car (*ETT* 12).

"Yes, They Must Have Been Blossoming Apple-Trees": I've taken the title from H.D's entry: "He read me William Morris in an orchard under blossoming – yes, they must have been blossoming – apple trees" (*ETT* 22). "Usury? *Usura.* Ezra was at one time, it seemed obsessed with this word" (*ETT* 22). The playfulness of "I love" and its sing-song do re mi fa so la ti do is an adaption of an early scene in *HERmione* (58–9).

"Rigor Mortis": H.D. speaks of "[s]ome sort of rigor mortis" (*ETT* 3) remembering her first kiss with Ezra Pound in the woods in the winter. "We are past feeling cold; isn't that the first symptom of *rigor mortis?*" Later in the same entry she remembers, "They used to say, *Run around, children; it's all right as long as you don't stop running.* Had I stopped running?" (*ETT* 4).

"These Roses, Those Thorns": Walter Morse Rummel was a pianist favoured by Pound. H.D. is reminded of the day Pound made public his plans to marry Dorothy Shakespear. This entry also is significant for H.D.'s recollection of the first time Pound used her initials and named her Imagiste (*ETT* 18, 40).

"You Spoke of Grapes": When pressed by Dr Heydt about her knowledge of Pound's reputation, H.D. relives her experience, "You are suffocating and I am hungry. You spoke of grapes somewhere – you were starving" (*ETT* 17). "I was TREE" is a variation on "I am the Tree of Life" (*H* 70), "I am TREE exactly" (*H* 73), and "I am TREE and I shall have a new name and I am the word tree" (*H* 119). George Lowndes returns to America, "Gawd's own god-damn country" (*H* 84).

"Magnolia": On 16 March 1933, Bryher writes to H.D., "N.D. [Norman Douglas] gives me lectures on how to make love – a damn lot of good it is to me. He is very down on the young English male, says as I do ... they wreck all their love affairs by laughing at the wrong moment and not being serious" (*AF* 104).

"Refusing Persephone's Bowl of Fruit": "Goodbye Dave, you'll come over Christmas Day, won't you?" H.D. quotes "Weekend with Ezra Pound" by David Rattray and is pleased that it seems "the first human personal presentation of Ezra" (*ETT* 19, 47). "But never Aphrodite" is adapted from Her's confession, "she was Queen of Love, never white Aphrodite" (*H* 173).

"Ins Rechte Licht": H.D. remembers Pound referring to poets around May Sinclair (a popular British novelist, poet, and suffragist) as May's "swarm of minnows" (*ETT* 9). In a surprise visit to her apartment studio with Richard and Ezra, they catch May with her hair in curl papers, but she remains the gentlewoman, and shows no signs of being upset by her early morning appearance (*ETT* 10). H.D.'s memory shifts in the later part of this entry to the summer of 1953 when she received an injection in her arm from Dr Erich Heydt. Encouraging her to record her memories of Pound, he questions her phrasing of Eva Hesse: "[s]he says it was to put you in the right light – *ins rechte Licht* – that he founded the imagistische Schule" (*ETT* 11). Peeling off another layer, H.D. recalls *Séraphita* by Balzac, "The Being, he-her, [who] disappears or dies in the snow. Séraphitus. Ezra brought me the story" (*ETT* 11). Jesus walked on water was inspired by H.D.'s letter of 15 March 1933, to Kenneth Macpherson: "Freud is just simply Jesus-Christ after the resurrection ..." (*AF* 100).

"Given to Unnatural Lust": "They say in Wyncote that I am bi-sexual and given to unnatural lust." H.D. writes quoting Pound (*ETT* 15). Recalling the rumours surrounding Pound and her father's reaction to the gossip, Dr Erich Heydt pushes H.D. further into memory by asking if she and Pound were "actually engaged." She quotes herself saying to Heydt, "how *German* you are –" when he asks about the ring (*ETT* 15–16). *A Lume Spento* was Pound's first published book in 1908.

"The Air Thick with Gadflies": H.D. admits that Pound introduced her to the writing of William Morris, including his "Two Red Roses across the Moon" and the "Defence of Guinevere," Emanuel Swedenborg's writing, and William

Blake's *The Marriage of Heaven and Hell.* H.D. also recalls the 1897 novel, *The Gadfly,* but can't remember who wrote it (*ETT* 22–3). Pound's signature also resembled a gadfly (*ETT* 25). It was around this time that Pound also refers to her as Is-hilda (*ETT* 23). Snipsnipsnip mimics Her's "clap, clap, clap, clap" (*H* 136).

"Sipping a Glass of Chianti": In her journal entry of 8 March 1958, H.D. recalls being gifted a painting from American abstract artist, Mr Morley, of a blue lion behind bars (*ETT* 6). In her entry of 9 March, H.D. writes that she and Joan look at the picture while drinking a glass of Chianti before dinner. Disagreeing with Joan about its image, H.D. argues, "I don't see the lion's head from here, this might be a Minotaur ... The bars are trees now. Will the lion devour me or redeem me – or both?" (*ETT* 7). Later in the entry she recalls seeing Pound in 1919 at the St Faith's Nursing Home when she is pregnant with Perdita. Carrying an "ebony stick like a baton," he pounds it against the wall and says to H.D., "my only real criticism is that this is not my child" (*ETT* 8, 30, 33).

"So Many Fishes, So Many Loaves of Bread": H.D. writes: "How many loaves and fishes are here? But we need not feed this multitude, not loaves and fishes. It is mostly apples. 'Pomona, Pomona. Christo Re, Dio Sole'" (Cantos 79 & 82 in *ETT* 33). Perdita Schaffner (H.D.'s daughter), quotes her mother: "People are in names, names are in people" (*H* xi). In *HERmione*, Her says, "People are in things, things are in people" (112).

"un-UNKing the UNK": In a letter to Bryher on 2 May 1936, H.D. wrote: "It is a long and slimy process, this of un-UNKing the UNK or de-bunking the junk" (*AF* xxxiv). H.D. is referring to the slow and painful process of Freud's method of psychoanalysis and his insistence on clearing the psyche of unhealthy associations (such as those H.D. absorbed in her family) in order to free the flow of creativity.

"Not in Her Lovely": This poem is based on a dream I had about Katherine Mansfield. Later, reading *Analyzing Freud*, I learned H.D. also called herself Kat and was frightened of having an x-ray.

"Angels Have Feasted": Curious to hear Freud's voice, I found a crackling recording with a few words on it. Since then, BBC has posted on YouTube Freud's only recorded transcript dated 7 December 1938, when he was eighty-one years old and suffering from jaw cancer.

"Newsreels": Bryher called her daily letters to H.D. "newsreels" filling them with humorous tales "of family and friends, monkeys and cats, books and magazines, politics and money, art and film" (*AF* xxvi).

"Wolf Is a Wolf": H.D. refers to her memory lapses about the *Cantos* as blackouts or "Chthonian darkness." From Pound she learned of the troubadours and Pierre Vidal who dressed in wolf-skins. In the early days of her relationship with Dr Heydt, he asks H.D. to explain what Pound means about "telling you to crawl out of your pig stye" (*ETT* 26–7 and *TFF* 206).

"His Head, a Pomegranate": H.D. describes Pound's hair as "wheat-colored," and he describes it as "a sheaf of hair/ Thick like a wheat swathe." Later in the entry she writes, "Bushel baskets of inseminating beauty fell upon barren ground" (*ETT* 36). Ezra compared H.D. to "a pink moth in the shrubbery" (*ETT* 38). H.D. refers to Canto LXXIX as the "pomegranate section" (*ETT* 39).

"Richard Mansfield's Last Performance": Pound took H.D. to a performance of *Peer Gynt* in Philadelphia in 1907. She recalls this memory when Dr Heydt presses her to reveal everything to him (*ETT* 20–1).

"Insane Always": Reading Canto xcii aloud to Dr Heydt, she quotes: "Le Paradis n'est pas artificiel" (*ETT* 31). Thinking of Pound she writes: "I could not *see* clearly but I could *hear* clearly, as I read 'm'elevasti/out of Erebus.' I could at least accept the intoxication of *Kuthera sempiterna* and the healing of myrrh and olibanum on the altar stone/giving perfume" (*ETT* 30).

"The Myth Can Not Be Localized": H.D. argues that "the basic myth can not be localized" (*ETT* 43).

"The Myth Turned": In a letter to Bryher and Kenneth Macpherson written during the beginning of her treatment with Freud, in March 1933, H.D. confesses to sobbing after the session and visiting "an old wooden place where they serve white wine and apples." She refers to the Wien and der Wein and "lilac time" (*AF* 35). H.D.'s dreams of a griffon who could carry her newspaper, 8 March 1933 (*AF* 53).

ACKNOWLEDGMENTS

These poems are conversations that I imagine H.D. might have had with Freud during her sessions in Vienna in 1933–34, and then long afterwards as she heard them replaying in her head. As recollections, they are written in air, "not written in blood ... yet written for all eternity" (*Bid Me to Live* 81). In a letter to her companion, Bryher, who arranged these sessions for H.D., H.D. describes Freud as "an old, old bird ... so old and so majic and so sweet" (Friedman, ed., *Analyzing Freud* 44–5). But the Professor unnerved her; she was "scared ... to death" and instead of speaking her mind, found herself "chirp[ing]" to him (*Analyzing Freud* 4). After completing her sessions, she compared Freud to "a bar of radium at the back of my head" (*Analyzing Freud* xxxv).

In the prairies where portions of this manuscript were written, magpies and crows tapped their beaks against my window. On one memorable day, a murder of crows gathered on the wires by the hydro poles and in the branches of surrounding pine trees. One swooped down upon a handicapped pigeon, decapitated it, and returned to its place in the centre of the line with the pigeon's head as a trophy. These black winged birds are messengers, and I remain open to their dialogue, like H.D., "listening far, far off, to echo of an echo; echo in a shell? What was [I] listening for?" (*Bid Me to Live* 15).

For a time I read H.D.'s *Collected Poems* every morning, then went for long run. The voices around or between lines of poems began to make themselves heard. Entering her "world of over-mind consciousness," I dared to follow, painfully recording, rerecording, correcting the translations I heard and was given.

Although H.D.'s early works inspired me with their urgency and energy, it was her prose, especially her biographical novels, *Bid Me to Live, HERmione, End to Torment,* and *Tribute to Freud,* that helped me find her and understand the "fiery moments" of her life. Susan Stanford Friedman's scholarship on H.D. and especially her book, *Analyzing Freud,* as well as H.D.'s tribute to Dr Erich Heydt, *Magic Mirror,* provided a further connection with H.D. and authenticated her voice. Discovering Michael Boughn's *Hermetic Divagations* soon after completing this manuscript gave me the courage to believe that a writer from Toronto could become another layer of story, why not?

I am indebted to my summer experiences at St Peter's Abbey in Muenster, Saskatchewan, where these poems were first born. Sporadic meetings with writing groups in Edmonton helped keep me on course and, after I moved to Toronto, the Long Dash Group patiently supported me during the writing of the dream sections of this book. Special thanks to Clara Blackwood for introducing me to the group and to John Oughton for his ongoing kindness. I am indebted also to Elizabeth Greene, whose copy of Barbara Guest's *Herself Defined* arrived when I wasn't sure if I should abandon this project or keep going. I was nineteen when I first read works by H.D. and Katherine Mansfield in a class on women writers at Queen's University. I am forever thankful to Elizabeth for enriching my world with their words.

I'm also grateful for the writing opportunities that led to the many stages of this manuscript: WIR at the Mackie House in Vernon, BC, and at the Al Purdy A-frame in Ameliasburgh, Ontario, where the silence of the lake and country helped me reflect on the poems. Even today I'm not sure whose dreams I recorded: H.D.'s, or mine, or a combination of both.

Grants from the Alberta Federation for the Arts (AFA) and the Edmonton Arts Council (EAC) helped me finish this book during a period of health and financial challenges. Without their support this manuscript would have remained between the covers of a binder, asleep and snoring.

As always, I owe thanks to my mother, Isabel MacLean, whose love and guidance gave me light in a world often filled with darkness and uncertainty. Her trays of tea and toast were a feast of good will and made all the difference.